**Published by**
**Phantom Publishing**
**2011**

This book is for all the dreamers that said we can and for the others that said we cannot.

# The Overture of Success

By:

James A. Amonett

"If you can dream it, you can do it."
– Walt Disney


"You may say I am a dreamer
But I am not the only one
I hope someday you'll join us
And the world will live as one."
–John Lennon


"Everyone has got to realize you can't hold onto the past if you want any future. Each second should lead to the next one."

–Joe Strummer

# The Overture for Success

1. Passion
2. Ethics / Integrity
3. Control
4. Innovation
5. Courage
6. Trust
7. Honor
8. Love and Commitment
9. Summary

**101 Quotes to Live by**

# Pas·sion   *noun* \\'pa-shən\\

## Definition of *PASSION*

1
*often capitalized a* : the sufferings of Christ between the night of the Last Supper and his death *b* : an oratorio based on a gospel narrative of the Passion
2
*Obsolete*: suffering
3
: The state or capacity of being acted on by external agents or forces
4
*a (1)* : emotion <his ruling *passion* is greed> *(2) plural* : the emotions as distinguished from reason *b* : intense, driving, or overmastering feeling or conviction *c* : an outbreak of anger
5
*a* : ardent affection : love *b* : a strong liking or desire for or devotion to some activity, object, or concept *c* : sexual desire *d* : an object of desire or deep interest

"Passion is something I pass on"

The first step of becoming a leader is to have a mission to achieve goals.

I keep a list of five goals with me at all times. If you don't, I suggest always keeping a list of your goals with you at all times. Having the goals with you is a great minder of what you want to achieve and where you want to go. Success is different for everyone; what you want and what the people around you want can, and usually is, two different things. When you make you list of goals, I'd suggest to start small and only write down five goals, three should be short term goals and two long term goals. Naturally, the long term will be more challenging. Achieving your goals should not be an easy task. It is <u>YOUR</u> challenge, regardless of the outcome. In the event a goal is not achieved, it is up to you to take it in stride. How you respond to the failure of missed goals, will help you learn for your mistakes and move forward.

My background is in management. I know when you are in a leadership position. some days you'll feel like you are being thrown into a lion's den. When you are tossed into the den you can learn a thing or two. Think about your normal day at work. Think about committing to a project (the lion), if you are prepared you can take care of the project and make it work for you.

Think about your last time you started something with passion. I'm sure your excitement was undeniable and manifested itself by smiling from ear to ear. How did it feel to have a passion? Now think about last time you failed. How did that feel?

You have two easy options, the easy way, which is to give up and fail, or long and winding road and increase your chances of success. Are we going to quit and fail or fight the good fight and succeed? As I look back on my failures, I realize that they are failures, because I threw in the towel, not because I was not capable to succeed. Sometimes in life, it is okay to run out of towels and fight when you feel like you have no fight left.

When you have passion and drive, there is nothing that can stop you. Three things are essential to keep you engaged; passion, drive and love. These three elements are the secret to reaching you own "success".

As you go down the road and keep going for your goals know that the drive to achieve your goals is driven by your passion. You need to feed your passion; you need to love what you are fighting for; love to work hard, love fighting and receiving the small victories, and love the people that helped you. Passion is going to keep going. Always have positive thoughts. Always believe.

Negativity spreads fast and discourages progress. Do not take part of negativity. Negativity is a cancer that is hard to be cured from.

Being passionate is going to take hard work. You can't fake passion. No matter how hard you try. Think of the things you have passion for. We ALL have a passion about something. Enhance that passion and you will enhance your drive.

You need to have passion inside of you to hit and reach your goals and dreams. If you feel you are starting to slip away from your passion, take a step back and keep positive supportive people around.

You can do it! Negativity will stand in your way but it is up to you to recognize it and eliminate it. It is possible that you have negative influences to deter you from your goals. The negative influences may not be malicious, but it is better to surround yourself with positive, supportive influences.

Think of it like this, when you are on a diet to lose a few pounds, it is very hard to get started. You start slowly then the next thing you know you are eating healthy, drinking more water and exercising a few times per week. Then you start to love healthy food and exercising regularly. Your initial goal to lose weight has proven successfully by your slimming waistline or sliding scale. The drive that kept you eating healthy has helped you reach your goal.

# Ethics and Integrity

# eth·ic

*noun* \ ' e-thik\

# Definition of *ETHIC*

1
*plural but sing or plural in constr* : the discipline dealing with what is good and bad and with moral duty and obligation
2
*a* : a set of moral principles : a theory or system of moral values <the present-day materialistic *ethic*> <an old-fashioned work *ethic*> —often used in plural but singular or plural in construction <an elaborate *ethics*> <Christian *ethics*> *b plural but sing or plural in constr* : the principles of conduct governing an individual or a group <professional *ethics*> *c* : a guiding philosophy *d* : a consciousness of moral importance <forge a conservation *ethic*>
3
*plural* : a set of moral issues or aspects (as rightness) <debated the *ethics* of human cloning>

"Rather fail with honor than succeed by fraud."

– Sophocles

# In·teg·ri·ty

*noun* \in-ˈte-grə-tē\

## Definition of *INTEGRITY*

1
: firm <u>adherence</u> to a code of especially moral or artistic values : <u>incorruptibility</u>
2
: an unimpaired condition : <u>soundness</u>
3
: the quality or state of being complete or undivided : <u>completeness</u>
<u>See integrity defined for English-language learners »</u>
<u>See integrity defined for kids »</u>


"Life is truly a boomerang.  What you give, you get."

– Dale Carnegie

A key component to success is having a strong will, knowing what to do and doing it the right way. Ethics and hard work is not a part-time job; rather it is a full-time job. Ethics is a constant *effort.*

Ethics is very black and white. You are ethical or you are not. You cannot be a little ethical. For the ones that have slipped a little off the ethics track, then there is one thing for you to do, do what's right, everyday. No Excuses.

How many customers, great teammates or family members have you hurt or lost without doing thing the honest way, the correct way?  Remember a white lie is still a lie. A small slip of ethics is still being unethical.  As someone once told me "you cannot be half pregnant" and you cannot be half ethical.

To help keep myself on track, I  think of the things that are important to me. What will my daughters, grandparents, mother, wife and co-workers think?  That should make the ethical decision very easy. However, I am not suggesting that you make what other people that of you a priority, but I am suggesting that you take their opinions into consideration as you are the one with an ethical decision.

The reason why I chose ethics and integrity for this chapter is they go hand in hand. Let's start with integrity.

Integrity is a very important trait for everyone to have. Regardless of your field work, integrity is part of the foundation for success, whether it is internal (within) or external (to the world).

Think of a time in your past. Think about the time in which repercussions of your unethical actions have lead to regret and / or shame. Depending on the type of decision and frequency, it is likely that you had a bad feeling in the pit of your stomach, paranoia, worried about getting caught. Then you start thinking about all the lies you have to create to keep the unethical. A lie is a lie. One of the great parts of being ethical is not keep up with your lies. Trying to remember what you said and did, to recreate the unethical actions. Sometimes in life the hard road should be traveled to ensure what is right over what is lucrative in any given situation.

Keep in mind that when ethics are thrown out the window and other people are aware of it, bridges can be easily dissolved and the hard work you have done is meaningless. Next time you are at the crossroad keep this in mind, what you are doing it for? Who is the emphasis of your ethical success?

# Con·trol

*verb* \kən-ˈtrōl\

## Definition of *CONTROL*

transitive verb

1

*a archaic* : to check, test, or verify by evidence or experiments *b* : to incorporate suitable <u>controls</u> in <a *controlled* experiment>

2

*a* : to exercise restraining or directing influence over : <u>regulate</u> *b* : to have power over : <u>rule</u> *c* : to reduce the incidence or severity of especially to innocuous levels <*control* an insect population> <*control* a disease>

"Never! Never! Never! Never! Give Up!"
– W. Churchill

Control is a touchy subject and means different things to different people.  Some people have control in different aspects of their lives. Being a "control freak" does not guarantee success. However, being out of control does not guarantee success either. Knowing how to take control of your life, professional career, employees, and other aspects of your life is essential.

The first step to acquiring contact is to know what you want to take control of. Next, make a list of small goals that will lead you to achieve your goal of control. As you achieve each small goal, create a more challenging goal. Remember your goals are your goals and belong to you.  You can only control what _you_ do, how _you_ act and how _you_ react.  It is counterproductive to try to control your employees, friends, family, co-workers, their actions and reactions.

Having control over other people essentially will diminish that person's respect for you. Keep in mind that being "in charge" does not mean to be controlling of other people.  If you are a controlling person, allowing leeway to other people will be challenging, but it is not impossible. Create a list of steps to follow to relinquish some control.  Trust in your employees abilities to perform their job and grow.

# in·no·va·tion

*noun* \ ˌi-nə-ˈvā-shən\

## Definition of *INNOVATION*

1

: the introduction of something new

2

: a new idea, method, or device : novelty

"Innovation distinguishes between a leader and a follower."
– Steve Jobs

It is often the case that someone wants to be first – the innovative idea that will put your company in its "cutting edge" status.  What is the difference between people like Steve Jobs, Bill Gates and the "Google Guys"? They set forth with their passion to achieve their goals without making any excuses. It is not an easy job from personal experiences; I can tell you that I almost lost everything to become an innovator.  I pursue opportunities that may have potential.  At times, the potential of that opportunity comes into fruition. Other times, the innovation does not get off the ground.

Innovators see a need or a problem, they have a vision and they solve it. Are you willing to roll the dice at an innovative idea? Are you willing to fight for your innovation at all costs?

If you get ideas in the middle of the night, at the dinner table, on in the shower, you are likely an innovator. If you think about improving a simple technique to get something done faster or better, you are an innovator. Remember that not all your ideas are going to be fruitful, or even good,  but you are keeping your mind working. One idea will lead to another. It may take hundreds of ideas to get a great one. Run it through people you can trust and be able to get an honest opinion.  Remember 99% of success is built on failure.

When you place yourself in a position to follow your innovative ideas, give your innovative ideas as much attention and care as you can.  Treat your innovative ideas like a baby that needs nurturing.  Keep your patience; live it, love it, do it!

# cour·age

*noun* \ˈkər-ij, ˈkə-rij\

# Definition of *COURAGE*

: mental or moral strength to <u>venture</u>, persevere, and withstand danger, fear, or difficulty

"Inaction breeds doubt and fear.  Action breeds confidence and courage.  If you want to conquer fear, don't sit at home and think about it.  Go out and get busy."

– Dale Carnegie

The very definition of courage states courage is a "mental or moral strength". It can be as strong or as weak as your mind or moral will allow it to be. The secret to developing the courage is to know you have it. We don't need to go visit Oz, we have it inside of us. We all just need to know how and where to look. Here's the deal about courage, we ALL have it. We just need to find where we put it.

I had a friend that had to speak at a funeral for a beloved family member. He had two choices. He could have ran away or ran with it. When he stepped up to the podium, he was in an emotional overload. He knew it was his responsibility to let people know how special she was, to him, during her short life. As he walked to the podium, he took a deep breath, walked up to the microphone and let the words guide him. After his speech, family and friends came up to him to tell him how courageous to speak. After speaking to him he told me that he could not, point with exact detail how he was able to find the courage to speak but, he wasn't afraid to do it.

That's the little secret about fear you have to face it. You can run away from it, but the fear will only grow. Face the fear and get past it. President Franklin Roosevelt said "We have nothing to fear, but fear its self". If you are in sales and you are afraid of the customer is going to say "no", guess what, customer are going to say "no", get over it!

Here is a little trick for you: In the mornings, look in the mirror and tell yourself "no" ten times or more if you would like. Get the "no's" out of the way. The more you do this the better you will become. I also suggest this for people who work in call centers making sales calls that are afraid of the phone. If you are afraid of something, try that something a time or two. Take control of courage you have within you. You will have the courage that you need. I know there are a lot of other fears, but there is always a way to face them. Don't like dogs, go to a pet store. Don't like driving, find a parking lot and making it happen. There is always a way to have the courage to fight your fears and achieve your goals.

"So to feel brave, act as if you are brave, be all of our will to that end, and a courage fit will very likely replace the fit of fear." – William James

# ¹trust

*noun* \ˈtrəst\

## Definition of *TRUST*

1

*a* : <u>assured</u> reliance on the character, ability, strength, or truth of someone or something *b* : one in which confidence is placed

2

*a* : dependence on something future or <u>contingent</u> : <u>hope</u> *b* : reliance on future payment for property (as merchandise) delivered : <u>credit</u> <bought furniture on *trust*>

"People are often unreasonable, illogical, and self-centered.  Forgive them anyway."

— Mother Teresa

Trust is the most valuable thing in the world. It is more valuable than the Hope Diamond and all the tea in China!

Trust allows you to believe someone else is capable and able of having your confidence. Trust is not easily earned or given in most cases. If trust is placed in the wrong person, or betrayed, disappointment, hurt and resentment can build.

There is also the possibility that someone can take advantage of other person trust. In most cases, people who have been taken advantage of, will not be very trusting mentality, trust may develop overtime.

Trust is an internal measure of protection, however heavily guarded people, will often will be less productive. For example, if you trust your team to help complete a project, the responsibility must belong to the team, and not an individual. Trust in the workplace is essential.  The largest challenge is surrounding yourself with people you can trust.

I am sure we all have many stories of people losing our trust. The important thing is once they are gone and out of your life, you have to forgive and forget.  I understand that will not be easy at first, but once you do, you will have a weight lifted. The dead weight of lost trust is too hard to carry, and will take a toll on your heart and soul. The most important thing is dropping the people that hurt us. Dust off, forget them, and move on. It is time to start over. Learn from your failures; remember your victories.

Trust is in every stage in life. It's in our personal relationships, co-workers, friends, family etc. It is imperative that you take care of the trust you are given as well as the trust you give.

Trust is the greatest gift anyone can give you and for you to give.

Trust your ideas. Trust yourself. Trust your passion. Trust your integrity. Trust your courage. Trust your innovation.

# <sup>1</sup>hon·or

*noun* \ ˈä-nər\

## Definition of *HONOR*

1

*a* : good name or public esteem : reputation  *b* : a showing of usually merited respect : recognition <pay *honor* to our founder>

"Honor is like an island, rugged and without shores; once we have left it, we can never return."

– Nicolas Boileau

Honor is one of those little words with massive meaning. Honor may not be achieved easily and once lost, it may not be easy to regain. In my opinion, the three main elements to intrapersonal success are honor, trust and love.

How do you gain honor? I feel this is something that may vary person by person. For me, it is as simple as being honest, hard work, and being ethical in everything you do.

The honor and respect you receive must be given back to that person.  You cannot expect one without the other. Practice what you preach. In friendship and in the office setting people's traits rub off on one another. Eventually, you subordinates will mirror their leaders. Let us analyses this: your team has a reputation of lying, treating the customers unfairly, coming in late and leaving early, gossiping, etc; why are they acting that way? Where did they get off track? Who is the ringleader of this negative behavior? These questions have an easy answer: it's due to leader's leadership, it's you. It only takes a few weeks for a team to mirror their leader.

Take a look at yourself. Are you sneaking in late and leaving early? Are you letting them get away with gossiping? Always remember employees mirror their leader. You have to remember words from management should be redeemed as gold. Do you want the gold that you give to your team to stay gold or do you want it to turn to rust?

I understand that these topics they have a similar resolution; however, you must remember how important these topics are for your leadership success. You need to know every day you cannot slip. You slip once and it will be held over your head for a long time. You need to act the part. If you do not act the right way, you cannot expect your team to act differently. At all times, you are being looked up to for guidance and leadership; you have to be there to take care of your team.

There are times it will be hard to lead properly, but remember this: if it is a personal issue, or anything that is not business related, leave it in the car. You need to be alert at all times to take care of your internal and external customers. Remember everyone you work with is YOUR internal customers and yes, that does include your team. Treat them with the same respect you would any external customer.

# Love and Commitment

# ¹love

*noun* \ˈləv\

## Definition of *LOVE*

1

*a (1)* : strong affection for another arising out of kinship or personal ties <maternal *love* for a child> *(2)* : attraction based on sexual desire : affection and tenderness felt by lovers *(3)* : affection based on admiration, benevolence, or common interests <*love* for his old schoolmates> *b* : an assurance of affection <give her my *love*>

"All you need is love."

- John Lennon

# com·mit·ment

*noun* \kə-ˈmit-mənt\

## Definition of *COMMITMENT*

1

*a* : an act of <u>committing</u> to a charge or trust: as *(1)* : a consignment to a penal or mental institution *(2)* : an act of referring a matter to a legislative <u>committee</u> *b* : <u>mittimus</u>

2

*a* : an agreement or pledge to do something in the future; *especially* : an engagement to assume a financial obligation at a future date *b* : something pledged *c* : the state or an instance of being obligated or emotionally <u>impelled</u> <a *commitment* to a cause>


"The Quality of a person's life is in direct proportion to their commitment to excellence, regardless of their chosen field of endeavor."

-Vince Lombardi

Love and commitment go hand and hand. They are very valuable in any and all situations in life. Simply put, if you do not love something, you are not going to care about it. It could be as simple as loving what you do or where you work. Lack of love leads to lack of commitment which will lead to distrust from your team. Remember that trust goes both ways: you towards your team and your team towards you.

When you are in a relationship without love every aspect in your life will be miserable. You will hate your job, your dog, your house, your kids and your spouse. Love, without personal relationships, leads to self contentment and self loathing.

Your personal life does affect your professional life, no matter how hard you try to keep them separated. It is up to you to determine which life you want to "fix" first if you are unhappy with both.

You may be wondering, "How can I get love and commit to something?" Love comes from within, but the challenging part is recognizing it. There are two types of love; good love and bad love. What bad love means is" loving" the wrong thing or someone detrimental to you. Drug abuse, drinking, overeating, and hording are a few examples of bad love. When self love is absent, the likelihood that bad love will take over is great. This is actually one of the foundations of addiction.

"How do I fix bad love?" Find out what causes you to have bad love. A great source to work on this is going to group meetings, find classes, see a therapist, or volunteer. To me volunteering is the most helpful; when you volunteer you get human contact and when you help with something you are interested in, you can start to grow. Over time the layers of not loving anything, and your bad habits, will slowly start melting away. Before you know it, you will start to love yourself and feel committed to something or someone else.

I know everyone has heard the phrase "You have to love yourself before you love someone or something else. " It is very true.

I believe love and commitment create passion. The quote I love is "passion is something I pass on." It may sound a cheesy but once you put the quote into action, you will realize how it speaks volumes.

This chapter may not help you with every aspect of your life, but when you do anything with love and committment, your life will positively change. The way your work will positively change and the way you treat others will change positively.

Bad love my come back from time to time, but you have the power to prevent it. If you are truly committed to your cause and yourself, you can beat bad love. It may be challenging but in time, it will become easier to accomplish.

The best kind of love to surround yourself with is good love. Good love may not come easily, but it is the most rewarding kind of love. Good love is the "positive" love; the support love.

Obtaining good love also takes love and commitment. Mainly, good love comes from loving yourself; loving who you are if you do not love something about yourself, you have the power to change it. Start surrounding yourself with positive people will allow you to achieve your desired change. If you do not have positive people around you, you have the power to change your support system.

Love is a feeling- a feeling of immense power. Commit to loving yourself first and keep in mind that love is not perfect, but it is capable of accepting flaws as well as qualities. Good love is understanding, patient and most of all unconditional.

# Summary

There is not magic pill to become a leader.  There is a saying "leaders are not made, they are born." I don't believe that at all. I think it is what we read, practice, hard work, exposure of great leaders and experience in life that make a great leader.

We are all given the tool box to be a great leader or great at anything.  If is up to each individual to be great at anything.  I have heard many people say that, "life is what you make of it."  The quote I very true and should not be forgotten.

If you are negative towards other people, ideas, and work, do you think you will be happy? I highly doubt it! There are times when it is hard to be positive; there are times you will work as hard as you can and there will be times you do not care. Sometimes, however, it is difficult to put failures behind you but when the stakes are high you have to.  Be a like duck, and let the water wash down your back.

From the topics previously discussed, I believe love is the most important. Love is to me more than a feeling; Love is very powerful. Love can make you do things that you never thought you could do. Love and passion will make the hardest tasks easy and then it can make the most difficult person understandable and manageable.

"All you need is Love," is the title of a great Beatles' classic. The Beatles are a great example of love and commitment. They were four young men that came from modest backgrounds. They knew they had something special and they had an amazing work ethic and talent. At the first time of trouble or first complaint against them, did they give up and put the guitars away? No way! They knew they had a commitment to excellence to be something very special. The Beatles had courage when they were young to leave England and headed to Germany, working tirelessly to make their dream come true. They worked to get it right and they surrounded themselves with the right people.

Everything has to come together in order to successfully their goals. None of us is perfect but we all have talent, passion, trust, honor, love, and commitment in each other to succeed.

Do I think you will be the next "rock star" of your industry? I have read a lot of the business books within the past few years. It is possible; it is up to you to make it happen.

What most of the books I have read shared was the idea that it is fairly simple to be great. I wish that was true. In life if you want anything at all you have to work at it; whether it is going to classes, reading and practicing your trade. If you don't like talking to strangers, change your ideology and talk to someone to get to know them. In a matter of minutes, that person will no longer be a stranger to you. Remember people love to talk, regardless of the subject matter, especially themselves.

Don't be afraid to ask questions; it will open you to new experiences and more learning. I often feel that every question that I have asked is "silly", but I learned and so did other people.

Most successful people will give you great pearls of wisdom and many will even keep up with you. I feel the care put into clients, projects and other people, in general, by successful people foundation of their success. Most successful people want to help other people succeed, instead of bringing people down.

Your life is what you make it. If you want "half effort" in life, then it will be a "half effort". All you want to do is bad habits; your life will become a bad habit.

Here is the million dollar question, "How do you want to be remembered?" We all want to be remembered for many positive reasons, but after a lot of hard work you will be remembered as a great father/ mother (if you have kids), a great leader, a great friend, a great son/ daughter. The two important to me is to be a great father and great husband. The rest will speak for itself when you are remembered in people's hearts and mind. I want to be someone who stood up for what was right and someone who did all he could for humanity. I left a few pages after the quote section for you to make notes on anything you want. If you have few ideas to do with those pages is write down your goals; write down who you want to be, long term and short term goals. Be sure to keep your goals in mind constantly and do what you can to achieve them every day. You have to be in it for you and only you. Life is what you make of it.

I know if you fight to make your life what you make of it, you will be a success. There is no question. You have to be all in for it to work, which is key. Nothing good comes easy and nothing easy is seldom good. Raise your bar in life and others will do the same.

In the next section is a section of "101 Quotes to Live By". I feel that there is something powerful in each quote and I look at theses quotes when I believe I am at the verge of a quitting, putting my life personal and they help me get back on track.

The very first step to get started is to make sure you put on a small piece of paper five short term goals, and five long term goals. I keep mine in my wallet. I think is a good place to keep it safe.

My first goal list read:

1. Get a new car
2. Get a promotion
3. Find a girlfriend
4. Learn something new every day
5. Be the best

I was 18 at the time and I am still working on the last two.

Well I got a new car around 8 months later. Six weeks later I got a promotion from a new department in my company. I started seeing someone around five months later. It didn't last, but that wasn't on the goal list. In regards to learning something new every day I did my best to learn something new about computer almost daily.

The final one, this took a lot of hard work (I think It gave me gray hair.) but we set the industry standard in our field. We were the best no doubt about it. Do I think this would have happened if I didn't have my goal list? I doubt it. To be safe I am glad I had my list and stood by it. You will never know how to play the game if you don't know what you are playing for. Since then, my prospective in life are a little bit different. I am turning a new page in life and I am going to focus my goals on my sheet in my wallet.

Starting a new way to look at life is not simple. You have change from inside and out. When you are ready to work on your "outside" image, dress the part. Dress as if you are going for an interview every day. In reality you are going for an interview. You are showing your co-workers and management you are a professional. Think about it if you and a co-worker were the same skill wise, you dress the part and the co-worker is in jeans and a polo shirt; who do you think is going to get the new position? **Look the part and become it**. You have the choice, and power to live with success. Too many people don't care and feel their life is a waste. Life is not a waste. Every person is special, important and unique. You are special and important. Life is not a waste. Make yourself know how special you are. Love yourself. Commit to being great. Commit to living ethically, with integrity, and honor. Love and commit to your family, your job and most importantly yourself.

# 101 Quotes
# to
# Live By

1. "Even if you are on the right track; you'll get run over if you just sit there."
- Will Rogers

2. "When the best leader's work is done, the people say we did it ourselves."
— Lau Tzu

3. "Learn to do what ought to be done, when it should be done and whether you like it or not."
- Roy Haley

4. "Nothing in the world can take the place of persistence. Talent will not; nothing is more common then unsuccessful men with talent. Genius will not; unrewarded genius is almost a proverb. Education will not; the world is full of educated derelicts. Persistence and determination alone are omnipotent."
-Calvin Coolidge

5. "A compelling vision tells who you are, where you are going and what will guide your journey."
— Ken Blanchard

6. "A manager is not a person who can do the work better than his team; he is a person who can get his men to do the work better than he can."
– Fred Smith

7. "How far you go in life depends on your being tender with the young, compassionate with the aged, sympathetic with the starving, and tolerant with the weak and strong.  Because someday in life you will have been all of theses."
- George W. Carver

8. "The trouble with most of us is that we would rather be ruined by praise then saved by criticism."
– Dr. Normal Peale

9. "As a manager you are not responsible **for** your team; you are responsible **to** your team."
- Unknown

10. "Do what you should do. Do it every time. Do it with every customer. That's how you create loyalty. That's how you sustain success. "
– Joe Calloway

11. "Forget failures, remember victories."
– Unknown

12. "Apologize, take ownership, and take responsibility to fix the problem."
-Peter Stark

13. "**Three Billion** people go to bed hungry every night; but **Five Billion** go to bed hungry for a simple word of encouragement and reorganization."
– Unknown

14. " As if you were on fire from within. The moon lives in the lining of your skin."
– Pablo Neruda

15. "The cream will quickly rise to the top but so will the gunk."
- Unknown

16. "Precision of communication is important, more important than ever, in our era of hair-trigger balances, when a false or misunderstood word may create a distraction as a sudden thoughtless act. "
– James Thurber

17. "We need to remember that miscommunication, poor communication or no communication can and will create incredible problems."
- Unknown

18. "Talk may be cheap, but the right use of words can generate in your followers a commodity impossible to buy."
- Alan McGinnis

19. "Effective speaking is not the result of eliminating those butterflies in your stomach, but simply getting them to fly into formation."
– Unknown

20. **"In almost any subject, your passion will save you.  If you care enough for a result, you will most certainly obtain it.** If you wish to be good, you will be good.  If you wish to be rich, you will be rich. Only then you must really wish those things and wish then with exclusiveness and not wish 100 other incompatible things just as strongly."
– William James

21. "You're either growing or your dying. There ain't no third direction."
– Thomas Callaghan II (Brian Dennehy) "Tommy Boy"

22. "If I know what you think, I would know what you are, for your thoughts make what you are. By changing our thoughts, we can change our lives."
– Dale Carnegie

23. "Throw every shred of negative thought into the consuming fires and slams the steel door upon your escape into the irresolute past."
– Dale Carnegie

24. "Only the prepared leader deserves to be confident."
– Zig Ziglar

25. "If our ideas are clear, the words come as naturally and unconsciously as the air we breathe."
– Dale Carnegie

26. "So to feel brave, act as if you are brave, be all of our will to that end, and a courage fit will very likely replace the fit of fear."
– William James

27. "Nice guys may appear to finish last, but usually they're running in a different race."
- Unknown

28. "A "seagull manager" is a manager that flies in, makes a lot of noise, dumps on everyone and the flies out."
– Zig Ziglar

29. "For a leader, every inaction may send a bad message."
– Zig Ziglar

30. "There is no pillow as soft as a clean conscience."
– John Wooden

31. "People with humility don't think less of themselves, they just think of themselves less."
- Unknown

32. "Never! Never! Never! Never! Give Up!"
– Winston Churchill

33. "I've got a theory that if you give 100% all the time; somehow things will work out in the end."
– Larry Bird

34. "Being miserable is a habit; being happy is a habit; the choice is yours."
-Tom Hopkins

35. "They may forget what you said, but they will never forget how you made them feel."
- Carl Buechner

36. ""Act quickly, think slowly."
– Greek Proverb

37. "It's not what happens to you, but how you react to it that matters."
- Epictetus

38. "If the mind of a man can believe, the mind of a man can change."
– Napoleon Hill

39. "We would accomplish many more things if we did not think of them as impossible."
-Charles Malesherbes

40. "Life is ten percent what happens to you and ninety percent how you respond to it."
- Lou Holtz

41. "There are only 3 colors, 10 digits, and 7 notes; it's what we do with them is important."
— Ruth Ross

42. "Attitude is more important than the past, than education, than money, those circumstances, than what people do or say. It is more important than appearance, giftedness or skill."
— Charles Swindoll

43. "Leadership is the willingness to accept responsibility for results."
— Brian Tracy

44. "Leadership is practiced not so much in words as in attitude and in actions."
— Harold Greneen

45. "Alone we can do so little, together we can do so much."
– Helen Keller

46. There are no office hours for leaders."
– Cardinal James Gibbons

47. "If we wait for the moment when everything, absolutely everything is ready, we shall never begin."
– Ivan Turgenev

48. "If you don't have the time to do it right; you better have the time to do it over again."
- Unknown

49. "It is better to believe than to disbelieve, in so doing you bring everything to the realm of possibility."
- Albert Einstein

50. "Whenever you do anything, act as if the world is watching."
– Thomas Jefferson

51. "Show class, have pride, and display character. If you do, winning takes care of itself."
- Bear Bryant

52. "Men willingly believe what they wish."
– Julius Caesar

53. "Average people look for ways of getting away with it; successful people look for ways of getting on with it."
– Jim Rohn

54. "The greater the obstacle, the more glory in overcoming it."
– Moliere

55. "Our greatest glory is not in never falling, but rising every time we fall."
– Confucius

56. "A great pleasure in life is doing what other people say you cannot do."
– Walter Gagehot

57. "No man is ever whipped until he quits in his own mind."
– Napoleon Hill

58. "Most of the important things in the world have been accomplished by people who have kept on trying when there seemed to be no help at all."
- Dale Carnegie

59. "It has been my observation that most people get ahead during the time that others waste."
— Henry Ford

60. "It takes time to succeed because success is merely the natural reward of taking time to do anything well."
— Joseph Ross

61. "There will be a time when loud-mouthed, incompetent people seem to be getting the best of you. When that happens, you only have to be patient and wait for them to self-destruct. It never fails."
- Richard Rybolt

62. "Genus is nothing but a greater aptitude for patience."
- Benjamin Franklin

63. "Patience will achieve more than force."
- Edmund Burke

64. "If you want to sing, you will find a song."
— Anonymous

65. "The ability to ask the right question is more than half the battle of finding the answer."
– Thomas Watson

66. "Success is the maximum utilization of the ability that you have."
– Zig Ziglar

67. "Sometimes it is better to ask some of the questions than to know all the answers."
– Unknown

68. "It takes less time to do the right thing, than it does to explain why you did it wrong."
- Henry Longfellow

69. "Rather fail with honor than succeed by fraud."
– Sophocles

70. "Faith in oneself is the best and safest course."
– Michelangelo

71. "I've learned only that you never say never."
- Marina von Newmann Whitman

72. "If you think you can win, you can win.  Faith is necessary to victory."
– William Hazlitt

73. "Faith is the refusal to panic."
– David Martyn Lloyd-Jones

74. "The greatest high you can get in life is by helping somebody."
- Timothy Stackpole

75. "If you want happiness for a lifetime- Help someone else."
- Chinese Proverb

76. "Inaction breeds doubt and fear.  Action breeds confidence and courage.  If you want to conquer fear, don't sit at home and think about it.  Go out and get busy."
– Dale Carnegie

77. "First ask yourself: what is the worst that can happen? Then prepare to accept it. They proceed to improve on the worst."
– Dale Carnegie

78. "The most important thing about goals is to have one."
– Geoffrey Albert

79. "The value of your goal is the path you take to reach it. The rockier the path, the stronger you'll grow. Move forward. Take Action, and make it happen."
- Unknown

80. "The only limitation in your life is the limitation of your own thinking."
— Unknown

81. "Great ambition is the passion of a great character. Those endowed with it may perform very good or very bad acts. All depends on the principles which direct them."
— Napoleon Bonaparte

82. "Men are like wine- some turn into vinegar, but the best improve with age."
— Pope John XXIII

83." The best thing about the future is that it comes one day at a time."
— Abraham Lincoln

84. "A person becomes a success if they get up in the morning and get to bed at night and in between does what's right."
– Unknown

85. "I pay no attention whatever to anybody's praise or blame. I simply follow my own feelings."
– W. A. Mozart

86. "Rather fail with honor than succeed by fraud."
– Sophocles

87. "Turning it over in your mind won't plough the field."
– Irish Proverb

88. "I am always doing things I cannot do; that's how I get to do them."
– Pablo Picasso

89. "There is no such thing as an accident; it is fate misnamed."
– Napoleon Bonaparte

90. "If you start to take Vienna – take Vienna."
– Napoleon Bonaparte

91. "Neither a lofty degree of intelligence nor imagination nor both together go to the making of a genius. Love, love, love and that is the soul of genius."
– W.A. Mozart

92. "Adversity is the midwife of genius."
– Napoleon Bonaparte

93. "All great performances start with clear goals."
– Dale Carnegie

94. "We define the total customer service experience as a consistent presentation and flawless execution across distribution channels and interaction checkpoints of the emotional connection and relationships you want your customer to have with your brand."
– Dale Carnegie

95. "When life gives you lemons, make a pie. Anyone can add the lemons to water and sugar but it takes someone motivated to make a change, to make something special, to turn it into something that they can be proud of."
- Unknown

96. "Innovation distinguishes between a leader and a follower."
– Steve Jobs

97. "Americans are overweight due to being fed bull crap their entire lives. "
- Zig Ziglar

98. If you think the grass is greener on the other side, then you need to start to work on your own backyard."
– Unknown

99. "A working-class hero is something to be."
– John Lennon

100. "The Future is unwritten. "
– Joe Sturmmer

101. Well, what are we waiting for?"
–Knute Rockne

# Notes

www.ingramcontent.com/pod-product-compliance
Lightning Source LLC
Chambersburg PA
CBHW051241170526
45165CB00004B/1525